The Management Guide to Selecting People

Kate Keenan

GW00367150

RR
RAVETTE BOOKS

Published by Ravette Books Limited
P.O. Box 296
Horsham
West Sussex RH13 8FH
Tel & Fax: (01 403) 711443

Series Editor – Anne Tauté
Editor – Catriona Scott

Cover design – Jim Wire
Printing & Binding – Cox & Wyman Ltd.
Production – Oval Projects Ltd.

An Oval Project
produced for Ravette Books.

Cover – The outer person may give a sharp
impression but the inner person needs to
be discovered.

Acknowledgments and thanks to:

Barry Tuckwood
Jeremy Bethell
Sue James

Contents

This book is dedicated to
those who would like to manage better
but are too busy to begin.

Selecting People

Managing people is not easy, but it can be made easier if you make sure that you have selected the right people in the first place.

When choosing new people, you are taking a most important business decision, because how you attract and retain them has direct implications on your own and others' work.

In a difficult economic climate such decisions tend to be a relative rarity, so it is important that you get it right first time. The penalties for making the wrong decision can be very expensive, not just in financial terms but also in terms of the time and energy which you and others will have spent in the process.

This book is about examining the processes you need to go through in order to select the right people, and making sure that you do.

1. Knowing What You Need

Some of the most catastrophic appointments have been those which were made in a hurry, with no clear idea of the important aspects involved in the job to be filled, nor what sort of person would be suitable for it. The need was simply to find someone. This approach is doomed from the start because it has three fatal flaws:

- It neglects to describe the job's key tasks.

- It fails to specify what sort of person would be most appropriate.

- It assumes that there was a job to be filled in the first place.

Deciding to Recruit

The decision to recruit is required in two situations:

- When a person moves on to a new position or leaves the company.

- When an increased workload indicates that a new job should be created.

When someone has left, the temptation is to look for another person just like the previous one. This is a mistake. Even before you decide to recruit someone to fill the gap, you should satisfy yourself that:

- You really do need to employ someone.

- You cannot distribute responsibilities between existing people.

- There is no-one to promote or to train from within the organization to meet your required needs.

Before you begin the selection process, you should carefully consider:

- If the vacancy you have to fill is necessarily the same job as has been left by the outgoing person.

- If there is now an opportunity to reorganize various duties internally.

If you decide that a new person should be recruited, you then need to decide exactly what the job is to be. Make sure you can identify how you expect the new job to contribute to the overall effectiveness of the business by considering such factors as:

- The extra value the job would create.

- The increased scope for improving quality.

- The additional services which could be offered.

Describing the Job

People generally have only a vague idea of the job they are recruiting for. Describing the job you want to fill is a key element in the selection process since it indicates precisely what you want someone to do. Every job is legally required to have a title. As most titles are not entirely self-explanatory, a job description is useful: it amplifies what needs to be done by the job-holder.

It is worth taking time to write a job description since it provides you with a formal record of what the job entails. If you can, consult with a colleague – two heads are often better than one in this type of exercise – and write down your agreed job description of the post you want to fill.

Job descriptions vary, but it is usual to list:

- The major tasks for which the job-holder will be held accountable;

- The chain of command (if appropriate);

- The extent of the responsibilities of the job.

Having a job description to give to the person who is ultimately successful will prevent later misunderstandings because the new job-holder will know the range of tasks to be performed. It also means that no aspect can be neglected simply because it is not liked.

Specifying the Person

Once you have a job description, you can write a person specification. Think about the specific needs of the job and the sort of person who would be able to do the work effectively. This is often the most neglected part of the selection process.

Most people can rustle up some sort of job description when this is requested. But ask for a person specification and you will be lucky to be presented with a few words on the back of an envelope.

This is largely because it is widely believed that the right person for the job will be instantly recognized the moment he or she comes through the door.

You need to write down the skills, abilities and characteristics you seek in the person required for the job, so that when you are interviewing people, you can find out how closely they come to matching your specification. It is useful to stipulate the required qualities under three headings:

- **Personal Requisites**.

- **Abilities and Achievements**.

- **Individual Characteristics**.

By identifying the personal qualities required to be effective in the job, it becomes easier to identify the sort of person who is likely fit it. For example:

Person Specification

Personal Requisites: physical make-up; special attributes; general circumstances.

For example:

- Manual dexterity – if delicate work is involved.
- Neat and tidy appearance – if meeting people or handling machinery is an important aspect of the job.
- Mobility – if the job requires travel at short notice.
- Upper body strength – if the job involves a lot of lifting.

Abilities and Achievements: general intelligence and special aptitudes; achievements, both educational and occupational.

For example:

- Numeracy – if working with numbers and manipulating data is necessary.
- Literacy – if the job involves working with words, such as preparing reports, letters, etc.
- Visual sense – if good presentation is paramount.
- Critical thinking and reasoning – if the ability to think things through and reach conclusions is important.
- Spatial and mechanical ability – if the capacity to work in three dimensions and to solve engineering problems is required in the job.

Individual Characteristics: disposition and personality; ability to influence; interests; level of motivation.

For example:

- Resilient – if the ability to withstand emotional pressure is an important quality in the job.
- Adaptable – if the job requires co-operation with other people.
- Persuasive – if it is important to convince others to accept ideas or buy products.
- Innovative – if the job requires the creation and development of new ideas.
- Resourceful – if making and implementing decisions is important in the job.

It is also helpful to distinguish between:

- **Essential** qualities: those which a person must have if he or she is to prove competent in the job.

- **Desirable** qualities: those which differentiate an excellent person from one who is merely good.

- **Undesirable** qualities: those which specify what you do not want. These are especially useful if you do not know precisely what it is you do want.

Separating the qualities you are looking for into these categories prevents you from looking for a 'Superman' or 'Wonderwoman' – who almost certainly does not exist.

Attracting People

If you need to advertise or use an employment agency, the person specification must be translated into copy. There is one trap to beware of. If you have only considered the tasks listed in the job description, an advertisement for a salesperson might read:

"… must be able to handle cash and know how to balance the accounts; must be prepared to work Saturdays."

If you have given some thought to the sort of person you want to do the job, the advertisement might read:

"… an enthusiastic approach to selling and an ability to get on with people is essential, along with a willingness to learn."

People select themselves in relation to the way the advertisement reads. For the first, you will get people who are attracted to the administrative aspects of the job, but who may have little or no interest in the selling aspects of the job. For the second, people will apply because they enjoy meeting people and selling, but may require training in administration.

If you have not included the key personal qualities you require, either you will be overwhelmed by the response or you will not get the right people applying. It is all too easy to say that there are no good applicants in the district when it could be the wording of the advertisement that was at fault.

In addition to your carefully crafted copy about the job, you also need to let people know how to apply for it and the date by which they must respond, e.g. 'Apply to Pat Jones by 25 July'.

Summary: Hunting Treasure

Selecting people is rather like going on a treasure hunt. You need to know what you are looking for. You also need to be able to recognize the treasure when you find it. So a methodical approach is important, which means that some care and creativity is needed in the way you get ready for the search.

Questions to Ask Yourself

Think about how you will go about selecting someone for the job offered and answer the following questions:

▲ Have I got a job description?

▲ Is this simply a list of duties or does it fully explain the function of the job?

▲ Do I have a person specification?

▲ Have I separated the essential qualities required from those which are only desirable?

▲ Have I discussed the specification with others?

▲ Have I advertised the job and if so, does my advertisement reflect the sort of person I am looking for?

If you can answer 'Yes' to all or most of these questions, you are more likely to attract the right calibre of people to apply for the job.

You Will be Doing Better If...

★ You have a job description for all the jobs in your business or profession.

★ You compile a person specification which identifies the sort of person you want for the job on offer.

★ You are clear about the essential qualities required for competence.

★ You know which desirable qualities would add to effective performance.

★ You use your job description and person specification to formulate accurate advertising copy.

2.   Gathering the Facts

The ideal result of your advertisement would be to get one applicant who is the best person to do the job. But this is rare. Depending on the job you need to fill, you will usually get more people applying than you can handle. So you need to make a choice as to how many, and which ones to see. The two are interrelated since it will depend on the quality of those applying as to how many of them you invite for interview.

Obtaining Advance Information

You need to get people to supply you with relevant facts about themselves. This material enables you to draw up a shortlist of likely people. For instance, too many previous jobs may be a bad indicator, just as living nearby could be a positive factor, particularly if the job involves a very early start.

There are several sources of information from which to glean the evidence:

Application Forms

You may have a standard application form or wish to compile one to send to people to complete. But remember, forms are generally designed to gather intelligence in an efficient way, and few people fit forms.

The information you receive usually only gives you the basic facts; it is unlikely to tell you what sort of person exists behind these facts.

C.V.s

C.V.s (or resumés) can provide information of mixed quality. Some are very detailed and tell you everything, including the mother's maiden name; others are too brief to be of much use.

The C.V. usually gives an individual's main educational and career achievements, along with some personal details to portray personality. Some people can look very good on paper, yet when they turn up, the whole impression can dissolve instantly.

A C.V. tends to provide you with more than an application form since it is the person applying who provides it, rather than you specifying what you want.

References

References are a way of obtaining an opinion of the applicant from a third party. The problem is that they are selective. If people are asked to nominate a referee, they are unlikely to give the name of someone who will not write a favourable reference.

If you decide to take up references, do so immediately (not forgetting to establish whether the applicant has let it be known he or she is looking for another job). Any delay may mean that the person has been appointed before their references arrive, by which time it is a bit late if the contents are not very positive.

Acquiring Direct Evidence

From the advance information you can decide whose applications you will process further. The best way to do this is to invite your chosen applicants for interview and/or assessment.

Testing

You may need to establish a person's disposition or abilities to perform certain tasks. A good way to do this is by testing. This can take two forms: psychological and practical.

Psychological (or psychometric) **testing** has become a popular way of assessing people, especially at executive level. These allow you to assess:

- **Abilities and aptitudes** – the specific technical and specialist skills which could be required in the job.

- **Disposition or personality** – the more detailed aspects of individual character traits.

It is important to understand that such tests can only measure an individual's potential abilities or personal preferences. They cannot measure whether someone is actually competent to do the job. However they can provide additional information which is not obtainable from an interview.

If you decide to use psychological assessment, you should make sure this is relevant to the job, and that the chosen tests are conducted by someone accredited in their use. The extra information obtained from this process should be discussed and explored further during the interview.

Practical assessment is the other way of ensuring that key skills are present. To do this you need to set up a simulation exercise to assess a person's competence.

Interviewing

Interviewing is the decisive stage in selecting people. It enables you to:

- Assess people's overall suitability.
- Explore previously gathered information.
- See how people respond.

Interviews have several advantages in that they are easy to set up, require little or no special equipment and take as much time as you are prepared to give. Most importantly, you get to see people and to talk to them face-to-face.

However, anyone who has been launched unprepared into an interview knows that it is more difficult than it seems. The main problems with interviewing are:

- Relying on first impressions. If you do not know what you are looking for, you can end up relying on your 'gut feel' (also known as the 'halo' effect) about people.

- Being unprepared. Unless you have done your preparation thoroughly, important areas for discussion will not be explored. As a result, people may not reveal their real attitudes until it is too late – often after you have already employed them.

Summary: Sorting the Evidence

Once you receive applications from people you need to sift through the information contained in them to assess which of them you will shortlist.

You can choose from a number of different sources to gather the facts about people. Decide which of these will provide you with appropriate information to determine who might best fit your specification, and choose which people to interview accordingly.

Questions to Ask Yourself

In order to compile a shortlist of suitable people from the relevant evidence, ask yourself the following questions:

▲ Did the right sort of applicants apply?

▲ Would references be useful in helping me choose whom to see?

▲ Have I made full use of the evidence received from those who applied to make a shortlist of the ones I wish to interview?

▲ If the job requires technical skills, will I need to set up a test for basic aptitudes?

▲ If personal characteristics are a key factor, would using personality tests assist in assessing them?

▲ If practical skills are a major part of the job, do I need to set up a practical test to check them?

▲ Am I happy with my shortlist?

You Will be Doing Better If...

★ You attract the right calibre of applicants for the job.

★ You use the information in their letters of application, C.V.s, etc., to make a shortlist of those you wish to interview.

★ You take up any references you think might be needed for specific individuals.

★ You consider whether either type of psychological testing could be of use and if so, you engage an accredited person to administer and interpret them.

★ You decide whether any practical tests are necessary and make arrangements for them.

★ You are happy about your choice of people to interview.

3.   Structuring the Interview

How successful your interview will be depends on how much information you can obtain from the people you meet, in addition to the facts you already have. If you feel you need to test anyone, it is a good idea to do so prior to the interview so that the results can be investigated at the time.

To make sure that nothing is missed in the interview, you need to have a structure.

Planning the Content

It is important that you have a comprehensive plan of what you want to discuss with each person. So first, you need to take a separate sheet of paper for each person and using the information submitted by them – letters of application, C.V.s, etc. – make notes of the points you would like to know more about.

Next, you need to plan relevant questions for each individual (which will contribute to providing a rounded and comprehensive picture of their character and personality) made up from six areas of investigation – current activities, working relationships, track record, personal interests, general circumstances and reasons for applying for the job – as follows:

1. Current Activities

Starting with the current job or activities is an excellent opening topic. Most people find it easy to discuss what they are doing at the moment, especially if they are asked unthreatening, factual questions about the things they do. For example, ask what they enjoy about their work, or (if unemployed) about hobbies and interests in general.

Discussing current activities breaks the ice and enables you to find out more early in the interview and appear interested and encouraging. Getting people to open up puts them at their ease and is best done by enabling them to talk about something with which they are comfortable.

2. Working Relationships

Eliciting attitudes about people's working relationships is a principle indicator of whether they will work well with others. For example, ask:

- How they feel about working with people.
- Whether they prefer working on their own initiative.
- What they have found stimulating or irritating in their past experiences of working with people.

This gives you an idea of their emotional ability to cope and co-operate with other people's demands.

3. Track Record

Exploring people's educational and occupational achievements gives you an idea of their willingness to learn and general flexibility.

If the individuals are school or college leavers or graduates, much of this part of the interview will centre on:

- What subject they enjoyed studying most.
- What extra-curricula activities they took part in.
- Whether anything undertaken at school, college or university led to something interesting or unexpected.

When interviewing older people, you need to concentrate on their previous occupations:

- What courses they have attended, and how these may have helped them to do their jobs more effectively.
- What they most enjoyed about any training or previous jobs.
- What they feel most proud of in terms of their personal achievements at work.

This allows you to see how well the information you have been given stands up to scrutiny. It enables you to compare what they thought they did with what they actually did. When applying for jobs, people tend to make their achievements seem more important than perhaps they are or were.

4. Personal Interests

Finding out more about people' outside interests and hobbies can show what motivates and excites them. There are both positive and negative aspects to this so you need to know:

- How much their outside activities reflect their abilities and act as a motivating force.
- How much their outside interests could take precedence over work interests, or whether a commitment to certain activities means that they would not be able to fulfil the duties required in the job.

For example, a keen footballer belonging to a Saturday league – who is applying for a job which may require work on Saturday – would clearly need to appreciate its full implications.

On the other hand, someone who is the leading light in a local club may prove to have just the organizational skills you are looking for.

5. General Circumstances

Handling general circumstances needs care. You do not want to be seen as a Peeping Tom, prying into areas which do not appear to have direct relevance to the job, but you do need to know something about people's personal lives. For example:

- What is their health record like; do they have commitments to ailing parents or to young children.
- How stable, or exacting, their home life is and if that could cause distraction and undue pressure at work.
- How mobile they are, and how willing they would be to attend training courses or work away from home.

When discussing such personal matters, make sure your questions are tailored in a manner directly related to the requirements of the job.

6. Reasons for Applying for the Job

Investigating the reasons why people are applying for the job gives you a good idea of what they expect from it. The significant questions concern:

- Why they want the job
- What they think they can bring to it
- What attracted their interest
- What their ambitions are and what they would like to achieve.

The answers to these questions can be most revealing. They can indicate which people have thought about why they want the job on offer and which have not given this question much thought. They can also uncover any discrepancies between what people think the job will offer them and what, in fact, it will.

If you do not ask questions relating to these six areas, you may end up making assumptions about what people would do in various situations – depending upon whether or not your impression of them was favourable. You could end up hiring people thinking them to be right – and then find out that they are not. Or you might turn someone down without ever discovering that he or she would have been exactly right for the job.

Summary: Interviewing Framework

Having a plan to work to when running the interview makes it more likely that you will ask key questions and not omit anything crucial. It allows you to present a professional and organized image when interviewing and provides a framework to ensure that you do not get side-tracked by interesting, but irrelevant, issues.

Planning the areas to investigate helps you focus on the information you should be collecting. It steers you towards forming a properly informed opinion as to the suitability of each person for the job.

Questions to Ask Yourself

When preparing for the interview, question whether you have covered the following areas of investigation:

▲ Current activities (as a way of opening each interview, in a way that will dispel nervousness).

▲ Working relationships (with colleagues at work or with friends).

▲ Schooling or occupational training (as appropriate).

▲ Outside interests (whether they complement or conflict with the job).

▲ Home and personal circumstances (whether they inhibit or enhance the person's ability to do the job).

▲ Reasons why each person is applying for the job.

You Will be Doing Better If...

★ You are thoroughly familiar with the information received from each person.

★ You make notes of the individual areas to explore in more depth from the information submitted.

★ You know what you want to investigate about each person's:

  – Current job.

  – Working relationships.

  – Education and training.

  – Outside interests.

  – General circumstances.

  – Reasons for applying for the job.

★ You have a detailed plan for everyone you will be interviewing.

4. Questioning and Listening

Having planned the areas you want to investigate during the interview, you need to extract the maximum amount of information from people when you meet them. If you are doing most of the talking, you are not getting their views or opinions. A 60:40 ratio in favour of those being interviewed is the one to aim for.

To get their thoughts and ideas, you have to ask carefully phrased questions.

Asking Questions

It is vital to appreciate why asking questions is so important when interviewing. This enables you:

- To obtain more information.

- To check professional knowledge relevant to the job.

- To explore views and opinions.

- To take control of the conversation.

By asking questions you can obtain information that has not been offered before and probe people's level of competence. More significantly, you are able to explore their opinions, attitudes and feelings.

Staying in control is even more important. As the

person who asks the questions, you put yourself in charge of the interview and ensure it goes the way you want.

However, asking just any old question does not get results. It is important to recognize that there are two distinct types of question you can ask:

Open Questions

Open questions are those which are open-ended and do not indicate a direction to take when answering. They usually begin with the words: Why? Where? When? Who? Which? How? (An easy way to remember them is to think of them as the 'W' questions.)

The strength of such questions is that people cannot answer you with a 'yes' or a 'no'. The answer has to be more explicit than that; even if it is as little as "I don't know". Sometimes even that response can provide useful information.

Open questions tend to be more difficult to ask. Most people avoid them as they are seen as intrusive, even threatening. But if you are to get information from people and allow them to speak freely, you must practise phrasing your questions in an open format.

For example, rather than asking "Do you live nearby?", re-state the question as, "How close do you live?" This will produce more information and allow people to expand their answers.

Closed Questions

Closed questions are those which allow people a 50:50 chance of replying with a 'yes' or a 'no'. They start with a verb, such as, "Do you...?", "Have you...?" and permit people to be monosyllabic when replying. These questions are good for checking things out, for example, "Have you ever worked with the public?" but they do not elicit much information.

If you ask closed questions you are unlikely to encourage people to talk freely. You could even get the impression that they had very little to say. If you rephrase the question in an **Open** format, you usually get a much fuller answer. If you are asking closed questions and getting only 'yes' or 'no' answers, you are making all the effort for very little in return.

Other even less useful forms of **Closed** questions can elicit other forms of biased answers; for instance:

- The **Limiting** question asks a person, for example, "Did you prefer French or History?" It might be that neither was a preference, but he or she is forced into giving an answer which may not accurately reflect their interests.

  If the question was rephrased as "What was your favourite subject at school?" the answer provides some useful insights into the individual's opinions and capabilities.

- The **Leading** question is the one which starts with opinionated phrases like "I presume you enjoy working on your own?" or "Obviously, you want a job that will let you use your qualifications?", where you are leading the person to answer in a pre-determined way.

- The **Multiple** question is a combination of all types of question. For example: "How did you get here; did you take the bus, or did you come by car?"

The **Multiple** question often gets asked because the first **Open** question was well-planned and probing, requiring people to think about the answer. During that silence less-experienced interviewers get unnerved and feel they have to fill the gap by asking another question – or several. These additional questions are usually **Closed** and so do not permit people to respond very readily to the original question – if they can remember what it was in the first place.

Try the six second test: time six seconds and ask yourself how long it felt. If you were interviewing, you would probably think it was an eternity. From the person's point of view, it would hardly seem long enough to formulate a sensible answer, particularly if the question was quite searching.

Multiple questions may also be a sign that you have not prepared what you wanted to find out and are using the interview as a method of preparation. Thus you are thinking aloud and reformulating your questions in front of people. If you ask unconsidered questions, you will tend to get hopeless answers.

Probing Questions

One of the most useful skills in an interview is the ability to ask questions which investigate the superficial answers people can give you. Their answers can also be too general. Questions that dig deeper will enable you to find out more.

Many interviewers find this awkward because it sounds as if they are prying. It is often tempting to help out the person who is struggling, by answering your own questions. This is counter-productive: you lose valuable interview time and you are unlikely to find out the answer to your question.

Be resolute: a good interviewer needs a healthy curiosity about people since they do not always know what information is relevant. Often, all you need to do is to say, "Tell me more..." and a talkative person will. If he or she is more reticent, phrase the question along the lines of, "You mentioned you found working in that area interesting. What would you say you found particularly interesting?"

It is difficult to prepare a list of useful probing questions because you can never be sure what a person will say. But a form of "Why is that?" or "What exactly did you mean when you said..." will usually allow you to find out more.

When interviewing, expect the unexpected. All sorts of information may not have been included in people's letters of application or C.V.s which is accidentally uncovered during discussion. Any useful supplementary facts can be pursued by asking probing questions. Sometimes, this may lead nowhere; at other times, it leads to interesting details. For example, the answer, "I didn't often meet customers in my job", to the initial question, "When have you worked with customers?" could lead to a fruitful avenue of inquiry.

The person who should do most of the talking in the interview is the one being interviewed.

Always follow your instincts. If you feel someone may have hidden depths, go on asking questions till you find out as much as you can. The ability to ask pertinent probing questions is an essential skill. It allows you to gather enough relevant information to make the correct selection decision.

Listening Skills

Once you have prepared and asked the key questions, it is equally important that you listen to the answers.

Listening is a great deal harder than it seems. It is

not simply a matter of sitting still and absorbing what people are saying.

First impressions can colour how much you are prepared to listen to people. If you like the look of someone, you are highly likely to listen more attentively. But if your first impression is not very favourable, you may be less interested in what they have to say. You need to beware of your first impressions. Try to remain neutral towards those you interview without judging them before you have a chance to hear what they say for themselves, or you could end up rejecting exactly the right person simply because you prefer blue eyes to brown.

If you have to listen for any length of time, you can find your attention wandering. This happens even if you are interested in what is being said because your interest will lead you to think of other related topics. While you are diverted, you cannot be listening to what is going on. If you are a relatively inexperienced interviewer, you will also find that thinking about your next question can distract you from attending to what a person is saying and you may easily miss a vital piece of information.

As an information processor, the human brain is a single channel and can only do one thing at a time, in spite of the fact that it does so in micro-seconds. You may catch the drift of what is going on, but if your mind is elsewhere you cannot pay full attention to what is being said.

It helps to know that there are two types of listening:

Passive Listening

Passive listening requires you to keep quiet and listen. You show that you are taking in what people are saying by:

- Maintaining eye contact – the best way of indicating that you are interested.

- Nodding at intervals – as a form of acknowledgement, which shows you are paying attention.

- Using phrases like, "I see", "I understand", "Really", "Mmm", "Uh-huh", "Yes", to encourage people to continue talking.

Active Listening

This is more taxing. It requires you to indicate not only that you are taking in what is being said, but also that you are evaluating what is being said. To help you do this effectively, you need to:

- Keep reminding yourself of the objective of the interview (to assess each person's suitability). This prevents you from getting deflected.

- Check any doubts about what a person is telling you, by asking a clarifying question. This gives him or her the opportunity to answer more clearly. If you do not test your understanding of what is being said, you may make incorrect assumptions.

- Summarize what has been said at various intervals during the interview. This will give you breathing space, time to think and to take stock. You will be able to evaluate what you have heard so far and what else you need to find out.

Summary: Interviewing Skills

Asking questions and listening to the answers are key skills in all management activities, but they are never so important as when you are conducting a selection interview.

It is essential that you phrase your questions precisely and carefully to ensure that you get the quality of information you have identified as necessary when you prepared for the interview. And it is just as essential that you listen carefully to what people say, probing their answers and finding out more.

Knowing Your Questions

To test your understanding of questions, identify what type these are – Open, Closed, Limiting, Leading or Multiple. Note the responses they may generate.

1. What do you like about working with people?

2. Are you punctual, or do you have problems with travelling to work?

3. Do you like to work alone?

4. Do you still live locally?

5. Presumably you'd like to work full-time?

6. Have you worked with the public before?

7. How do you get on, when handling money?

8. Would you like to work outside or in the office?

9. Obviously you like working with systems?

10. Have you worked under pressure, and are you used to dealing with difficulties or not?

You Will be Doing Better If...

You listen to what people say and ask probing questions to find out more. Here are some answers to a question about dealing with people, all containing clues to investigate. Think of the **questions** you would ask to follow up these **answers**:

- I quite like meeting new people.

- I used to meet lots of people.

- I don't often meet people these days.

- I always try to be as pleasant as I can.

- I find people easier to deal with now.

Answers which include words like 'quite', 'used', 'often', 'try', 'now', should trigger your interest and provoke a probing question. Make sure that the probing question you ask is an open question which elicits more information.

Answers to page 40. Q1. = Open; Q2. = Multiple; Q3. = Multiple; Q4. = Closed; Q5. = Leading; Q6 = Closed Q7. = Open; Q8 = Limiting; Q9 = Leading; Q10 = Multiple.

5.   Interviewing

Conducting successful interviews requires a little advance organization if you are to get the best from the time you spend interviewing. If you think that you can play interviews by ear because you have already done a few, you will present people with the idea that you cannot be bothered.

Managing Interviews

It is important to think about how each interview will be managed. A rehearsal would not come amiss if you have not interviewed before. It could help you to feel more comfortable in the interviewer's role. Have a dry run with a colleague, a member of the family, or a tape recorder.

It is a good idea to consider interviewing in pairs. Having two interviewers requires extra management and in this case one interviewer should act as the 'Controller-cum-Organizer'. (This does not necessarily have to be the most senior person of the two.)

You should agree who will be asking questions about what topics – otherwise neither party will be quite sure just who does what. It is a good idea to ask questions and take notes by turn. It also helps if both interviewers, when concluding their topics, invite each other to pose any additional questions he or she may have in case one or other has missed a pertinent question or failed to probe an answer deeply enough.

If there is more than one interviewer, the one who opens an interview should also be the one who closes it. That way, everybody knows that the interview is over, the individual is free to go, and the interviewers can move on to the next interview.

If you are holding interviews in an office, make sure you are not disturbed. If you do not secure privacy, the odds are that when you have asked a searching question and someone is about to 'spill the beans', you will be interrupted. You may never get back to that moment.

Whatever method is chosen, make sure the relevant papers are to hand – i.e. job description, person specification, C.V.s and record sheets, and plenty of pens and paper, just in case.

Timing Interviews

Considerations about the timing of the interview are:

- What day or days you will devote to interviews.
- How long you want the interviews to last.

Pace the interviews over a set period and try not to do more that six in any one day, or you will find it difficult to remember who you have interviewed.

You may also have to interview well into the evening or early in the morning since it is difficult for many people to get away from their current jobs during working hours. Also, allow for travelling time; for example, 11 o'clock is better than 9 o'clock if someone has a long journey to get to the interview.

Running Interviews

There are some basic principles to observe when running an interview, and these are:

1. **Welcoming** candidates and **checking** that you have the right person. (It has happened that the wrong person was interviewed just because the name was never checked.) Creating the right atmosphere from the start allows people to settle in rapidly to an unfamiliar situation. It often requires no more than simple courtesies, such as shaking hands, smiling and a few pleasantries about the weather, to make them feel at ease.

2. **Introducing** the interview by briefly **explaining** its purpose and what you propose to do. If there are two of you, indicate the areas of the discussion each will control. Mention that you have other people to see and that notes will be taken to ensure you have an accurate record of the discussion.

3. **Using** your interview plan for topics for discussion. Start with easy factual areas, such as current job or hobbies. Getting people to talk early in an interview as this will dispel any nervousness. Keep areas you wish to probe more deeply for later, after they have relaxed and are willing to talk.

4. **Interviewing well**. To create rapport you need to be friendly but purposeful and constantly remind yourself that you are there to get the most out of people. You also need to:

- **Keep an open mind** about each person you meet. If you make up your mind immediately, without finding out more, you may find your behaviour reflects your instant opinion.

- **Let people talk**. The interview is a two-way conversation. If you do most of the talking, you will get less information. You also give the impression that you are only interested in yourself.

- **Be flexible**. When you are carrying out interviews, no matter how careful your preparation, someone may produce unexpected information which does not fit with what you planned to discuss. If this happens, be willing to abandon that part of your plan and follow the trail which now seems more promising.

- **Maintain eye contact**. Letting people know that you are giving them your full attention is best done by eye-to-eye contact.

- **Listen carefully**. Remember the pitfalls of making assumptions which can happen if you do not listen carefully. A useful ditty states: "If I ASSUME something about someone else, I not only make an ASS out of U, but also of ME." In other words, both parties end up feeling foolish.

5. **Telling** people about the job – but briefly. It is unlikely that all the details will be remembered, but make sure that you mention:

- Salary; how much will be paid and when.

- Holiday entitlement; will this year's holidays be honoured.

- Hours of work; what times, days, shifts, etc.

If you do not tell people these key facts about the job, when you ask them if they have any questions, they will invariably ask you about Pay, Holidays and Working Conditions. If these are the only questions a person asks you, you are likely to conclude that the only thing he or she is interested in is Pay, Holidays and Working Conditions, which could lead you to an unfair conclusion.

6. **Finishing** the interviews by asking people if they have any questions to ask you about the job or company. Conclude by thanking them for attending, and saying when you will be letting everyone know the results – and make sure you do.

Never tell someone at the close of the interview that he or she has got the job. You need time to assess all those you have seen, even though one person may appear to be an obvious choice. The decision as to whom to appoint should be made outside the charged atmosphere of the interview. In addition, if you make a spontaneous verbal offer of employment, it is taken in law as a binding contract. Should you subsequently withdraw it, the individual concerned has a right to sue for breach of contract.

Allow time between each interview to complete and organize the notes you have been taking during your discussions. If you do not do so, and think you can rely on your memory to recall certain details, you will almost certainly get it wrong. "You know, the redhead who collects wine labels." "Don't you mean the one who likes free-fall parachuting?"

It is on the information you obtain from interviews that you will base your decisions as to how suitable each person is for the job. It is therefore vital that your notes are accurate and comprehensive.

Respecting People

The selection process itself is fairly nerve-racking. Treat those you interview as interesting human beings who are looking for the right situation in life, rather than cannon fodder for the position you have to fill. Make sure that you:

- **Keep your interviews on schedule**. If you keep people waiting you may give the impression that you are not very organized – an impression which may result in their deciding that this may not be the organization for them. If you are running late, let them know and indicate the reasons for the delay.

- **Seat them comfortably**. Placing people in an inferior position does not do much to create rapport and may intimidate them.

- **Keep a balanced style**. Getting involved in an alternate 'nice' and 'nasty' interview style, either alone or with a colleague, is counter-productive because it leaves people feeling bullied and bewildered.

- **Ask relevant questions**. Thinking up and asking trick questions is a futile activity because the answers only prove that the individual does not know the answer to that question. Also, make sure you avoid questions of a discriminating nature, such as: "Do you intend to have children?"

- **Offer people their expenses**. Expenses are a small part of the cost of selecting, but this could be a substantial burden for those invited for interview. By paying expenses, you indicate that you value them.

Summary: Interviewing Effectively

In order to interview effectively, it is important to work out in advance how the proceedings will be managed.

Managing interviews requires preparation, especially if there are two people involved, because the areas for discussion need to be carefully allocated.

Tackling interviews requires an organized and business-like approach. It requires you to concentrate whole-heartedly on the questions and the responses, while remaining objective throughout.

Treating people with courtesy and respect is good manners. It also sets the tone and epitomizes the attitudes of the company you represent.

Questions to Ask Yourself

Review your performance as an interviewer by answering the following questions.

▲ Did I ensure the venue was comfortable and free from interruptions?

▲ Did I enable people to settle down at the start of the interview so that they could give of their best?

▲ Did I ask the right type of questions?

▲ Did I give people full opportunity to reply to my questions and have their say?

▲ Did I listen carefully to their answers and follow up significant phrases when they occurred?

▲ Did I give them the information they needed about the job?

▲ Did I allow sufficient time between interviews to review and make orderly notes?

You Will Be Doing Better If...

★ You hold the interviews in a private and comfortable place.

★ You do not see too many people in one day.

★ You make people feel welcome and get them talking from the start.

★ You give each of them your undivided attention.

★ You tell them about the job on offer.

★ You give them a chance to ask any questions they have.

★ You obtain enough information about each person to form an excellent idea of their character and capabilities.

★ You allow sufficient time between interviews to review their responses and collate your notes.

★ You manage your interviews well.

6.   Assessing the Evidence

Once the interviews are completed, you need to rate people in a way that allows the fair comparison of everyone you have seen. The best way to do this is to assess how closely each person matches the specification for the job.

Rating People

As an aid to making your decision it is useful to have some form of rating scale which gives people a score for each area of the specification. Concentrate on those qualities designated as essential, and rate each person you have interviewed according to how closely they fit your specification. For instance:

8 – 10 **Definitely Yes**; this person fully fits the specification for this area.

7 – 5 **Possible**; there are some slight discrepancies between the person and the specification.

4 – 2 **Unlikely**; there are major areas where this person does not fit the specification.

1 – 0 **Definitely No**; this person does not fit the specification at all.

It is important to realize that not every characteristic is as important as the others. You could, for example, mark the less vital qualities or attributes out of 10; the more important ones could be marked out of 20 or even 30, depending on how essential that attribute is to successful performance in the job.

By adding up these scores, you can work out an order of merit. This method of rating people allows you to compare everyone you see on the same basis.

Weighing the Pros and Cons

Having amassed the information, it is time to make a choice. When you have completed all the interviews, go through the individual assessments and list each person in order of how closely he or she matched your specification.

Sometimes an individual can stand out head and shoulders above the others but, more often, things are not so straightforward.

- **So/So People**. Should you find yourself with people who merit only a 'possible' rating, ask yourself seriously whether you wish to make an appointment. It might be more prudent to live with the vacancy until you can find better applicants, rather than take on someone who lacks some of the requisite 'essential' qualities. Go back to the person specification and make sure that it is realistic in defining the sort of person who would be competent in the job – and that you are not looking for the impossible.

- **Equal People**. If, say, you have someone who registered 67 out of a 100, and another whose points add up to 32, there is not much debate about who is the most suitable. If you find you have two people who are roughly neck and neck on essential qualities, scoring, say, 64 and 66, then which one to choose perhaps rests more on how he or she measures up to the desirable qualities. And in the event of a dead heat, which one you choose may rest on personality and your own personal preference.

- **Needful People**. If you find out that someone is in desperate need of a job, do not let your sympathy for their circumstances influence your decision, unless they fit your person specification. (Feeling that a person deserves a chance is not a reason to offer a job.) On the other hand, do not dismiss someone whose disability might at first seem to preclude them. (They may turn out to fulfil all other requirements of the job description.) Being in a wheelchair or having a hearing problem does not preclude someone from being a computer whiz.

If there are no really suitable people for the job, do not be afraid to go back to the drawing board and start the whole selection process again.

If you have any reservations about the person you have chosen, write them down and think about them. If these concern a lack of specific skills or expertise, this can be rectified by training. Lack of experience can also be resolved by giving on-the-job instruction and advice.

Summary: Making the Right Choice

When appointing someone you are making an important decision which has long-lasting implications for yourself, your business or any other people involved. It is critical to correlate information from those you have interviewed with the person specification.

It is also essential that you remain objective and keep sentiment out of the decision as to whom to appoint. Keeping the decision-making process logical and rational will help you choose the best possible person for the job.

Check List for Selecting People

If you are finding that selecting people proves more difficult than you thought, think about whether it is because you have failed to take account of one or more of the following aspects:

Knowing What You Need

If you do not take the time to describe the job you have on offer nor specify what sort of person you need to fill the post, you will almost certainly not attract the right people. You need to have spent time on this part of the process and, if possible, to have done it in conjunction with someone else. Without a good job description and a well-defined person specification you cannot expect to advertise effectively nor attract the right calibre of people.

Investigating People

If you have not taken the time to read and absorb the information provided by applicants, you may not call the right people for interview. Nor will you know which are the relevant details to investigate in order to assess each person's suitability.

Managing the Interview Properly

If you did not plan a formal structure for the interview, you could have ended up 'playing it by ear'. If there were two of you interviewing and you did not agree the framework, it could have been a bit of a shambles. If not enough notes were made or insufficient time was allowed between interviews for collating them, you may not remember who was who.

Asking the Right Questions

If you have not identified at least one person who is right for the job, you may not have asked the right form of questions. You need to make sure you ask open questions (which elicit information), not closed ones. If you did not ask probing questions, you may not have obtained all the information you should have. It could be that you did not think carefully enough about how you phrased your questions, or that you did all the talking.

Assessing People

If you find yourself speculating as to whether someone will be right or wrong for the job, you very probably do not have enough information on which to base a decision. Having a correct specification will ensure that you know you are looking for the right person in the first place, and having a rating scale to assess each individual ensures that you are able to remain objective and that you do not allow first impressions to colour your choice.

The Benefits of Selecting the Right People

Selecting new people is a time-consuming process. How you go about choosing them plays an important part in retaining them. The process is expensive in time and resources, so it is a good investment to prepare properly and give it the attention it deserves.

The right person will contribute considerably to the success of the whole concern. Selecting an individual who is productive and highly motivated will influence others in a positive way, alleviating pressure and reviving morale.

Making the wrong choice can result in all sorts of problems. If everyone has been working long and hard to make up the deficiency an absence has brought about, choosing the wrong person can demoralize those who have been covering the gap and set them back even further.

The wrong person can be a liability. The right person will be an asset. It is worth the effort to get it right.

Glossary

Here are some definitions relating to Selecting People.

Active listening – Asking further questions to clarify responses to initial questions.

Advertisement – Well-ordered bait for attracting suitable prey.

Applicants/Candidates – Those who present themselves as suitable for the job on offer. It does not mean they are.

Application forms – Aids to compiling a shortlist, only as useful as the information requested.

Assessing – Making a judgement using pre-specified criteria.

Assuming – Jumping to conclusions without evidence, usually with fatal results.

Characteristics – The distinguishing qualities which make a person unique.

Closed questions – Those which allow people to answer 'Yes' or 'No'; only good for checking facts.

C.V. (*Curriculum Vitae*) – Life History; and some of them are.

Decision – Conclusion reached after deliberation of all available evidence.

Desirable qualities – Factors which will prove an added bonus in the job.

Employment agency – Useful short cut to the short-list.

Essential qualities – Basic requirements for competent performance.

General circumstances – Personal factors which could affect the ability to do the job.

'Gut feel' – Instinctive response as opposed to objective evidence. A sensation to be avoided.

Job description – List of core tasks which make up a job. Make sure that it is realistic.

Interests – Information which gives an extra dimension to an individual's personality.

Interview – A two-way conversation, not the third degree.

Open questions – Those which allow people to express views; good for obtaining information.

Passive listening – Nodding and making noises to show you are taking in what is being said.

Person specification – Vital list of qualities of the sort of person you are looking for.

Psychological testing – Assessment of personality or aptitudes.

Probing questions – Those which elicit deeper detail and often uncover things that people would not think to tell you.

Rapport – Apparent empathy between the individual and the interviewer.

References – Other people's opinions of someone's abilities. To be treated with caution.

Resumé – Personalised summary of skills.

Selecting – Weeding out the right from the wrong.

Shortlist – Limited selection of the best of the bunch.

The Author

Kate Keenan is a Chartered Occupational Psychologist with degrees in affiliated subjects (B.Sc., M.Phil.) and a number of qualifications in others.

She founded Keenan Research, an industrial psychology consultancy, in 1978. The work of the consultancy is fundamentally concerned with helping people to achieve their potential and make a better job of their management.

By devising work programmes for companies she enables them to target and remedy their managerial problems – from personnel selection and individual assessment to team building and attitude surveys. She believes in giving priority to training the managers to institute their own programmes, so that their company resources are developed and expanded.

Although aware of the pitfalls, she never finds selecting people easy. This is largely because when interviewing likely contenders her main problem is not that too little information is gathered, but too much.

THE MANAGEMENT GUIDES

Available now at £2.99 each:

Making Time ☐

Managing ☐

Managing Yourself ☐

Planning ☐

Selecting People ☐

Solving Problems ☐

To be published in July 1995:

Communicating ☐

Delegating ☐

Meetings ☐

Motivating ☐

Negotiating ☐

Understanding Behaviour ☐

¬These books are available at your local bookshop or newsagent, or can be ordered direct. Prices and availability are subject to change without notice. Just tick the titles you require and send a cheque or postal order for the value of the book to:

B.B.C.S., P.O. Box 941, HULL HU1 3VQ (24 hour Telephone Credit Card Line: 01482 224626), and add for postage & packing:

UK (& BFPO) Orders: £1.00 for the first book & 50p for each additional book up to a maximum of £2.50.
Overseas (& Eire) Orders: £2.00 for the first book, £1.00 for the second & 50p for each additional book.